ORIGINAL MOTION PICTURE SOUNDTRACK

LITTLE SHOP OF HORRORS

PROLOGUE
(LITTLE SHOP OF HORRORS)

Words by
HOWARD ASHMAN

Music by
ALAN MENKEN

Medium Rock 'n' Roll beat

6

Shang - a - lang, feel __ the sturm and drang in the air. __

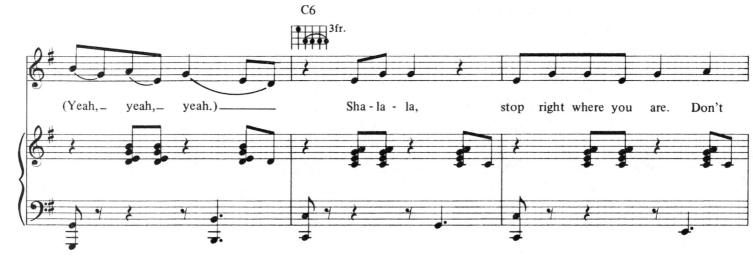

(Yeah, __ yeah, __ yeah.) __ Sha - la - la, stop right where you are. Don't

move a thing. __ You bet - ter, you bet - ter,

tell - in' you you bet - ter tell your ma - ma some - thin's gon - na get her.

SKID ROW
(DOWNTOWN)

Words by
HOWARD ASHMAN

Music by
ALAN MENKEN

DA-DOO

Words by
HOWARD ASHMAN

Music by
ALAN MENKEN

GROW FOR ME

Words by
HOWARD ASHMAN

Music by
ALAN MENKEN

Moderately, in 2

I've giv-en you sun - shine.
plant food

I've giv-en you dirt.
and wa-ter to sip.

You've giv-en me noth - in'
I've giv-en you pot - ash.

but heart - ache and hurt.
You've giv-en me zip.

I'm beg-gin' you sweet - ly.
Oh God, how I mist you!

I'm down on my knees.
Oh pod, how you tease!

live. I've tried you at lev-els— of mois-ture from des-ert— to

mud. I've giv-en you grow-lights and min-er-al sup-ple-ments. What do you want from me?

Blood? I've giv-en you sun - light.— I've giv-en you rain.

Looks like you're not hap-py— 'less I o-pen a vein.—

I'll give you a few drops if that-'ll ap - pease.

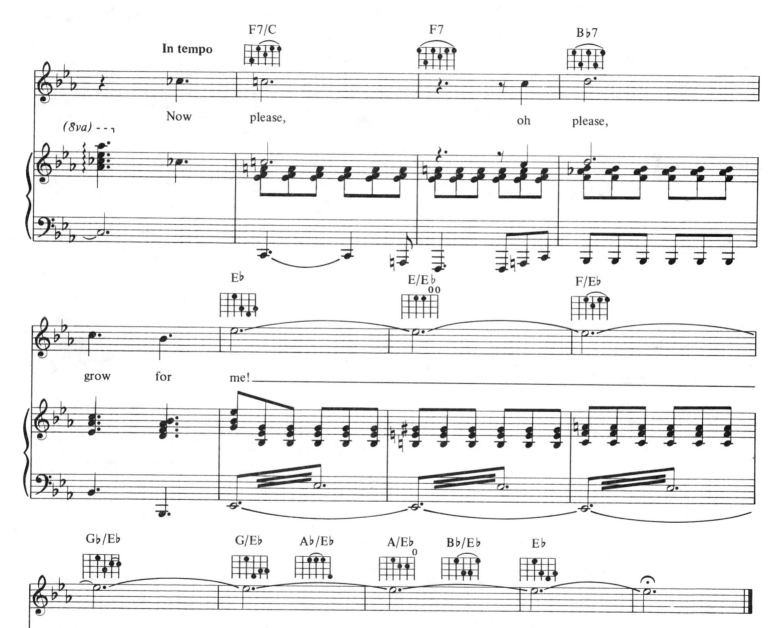

Now please, oh please,

grow for me! _____

SOMEWHERE THAT'S GREEN

Words by
HOWARD ASHMAN

Music by
ALAN MENKEN

snug-gle watch-in' Lu-cy on our big, e-nor-mous twelve-inch screen. I'm

Coda

Far from Skid Row,

freely

I dream we'll go some-where that's

a tempo

green.

SOME FUN NOW

Words by
HOWARD ASHMAN

Music by
ALAN MENKEN

now, (Good God, the boy.)___ he's hav - in' some fun now. (Oh boy, oh boy.)___ Yes,___

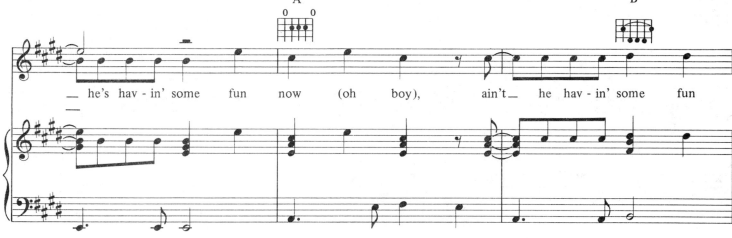

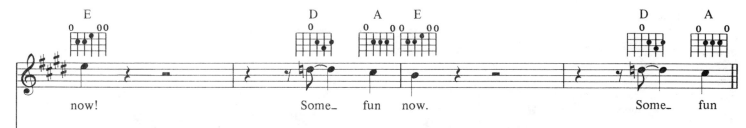

___ he's hav - in' some fun now (oh boy), ain't___ he hav - in' some fun

now! Some___ fun now. Some___ fun

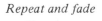

Repeat and fade

now. Some___ fun now. Some___ fun

DENTIST!

Words by
HOWARD ASHMAN

Music by
ALAN MENKEN

Bumbling botanist Seymour Krelborn (RICK MORANIS) discovers a plant that could devour the world.

Mushnik the florist (VINCENT GARDENIA, center) embraces his favorite employees — beautiful, put upon Audrey (ELLEN GREENE, left) and bashful blundering Seymour (RICK MORANIS, right) — unaware that their innocent potted plant will flower into a botanical Dracula.

Ronette (MICHELLE WEEKS, left), Chiffon (TISHA CAMPBELL, center) and Crystal (TICHINA ARNOLD, right) amble past Mushnik's Skid Row flower shop, where a budding plant vampire is making business boom. The singers serve as a street-smart "Greek chorus" who underscore the action in the monster comedy with music.

Skid Row florist Mushnik (VINCENT GARDENIA, right) demands an explanation from his wimpy salesclerk Seymour (RICK MORANIS, left) for the strange, slurping noises in the cellar of the "Little Shop of Horrors."

Dee-jay Weird Wink Wilkenson (JOHN CANDY) talks to his listeners about Seymour Krelborn's (RICK MORANIS) strange exotic plant discovered during a total eclipse of the sun.

JAMES BELUSHI (left) makes a cameo appearance as a high-powered hustler who hopes to get rich by selling the "cuttings" from Seymour's (RICK MORANIS, center) sinister plant while Audrey (ELLEN GREENE) nervously watches.

Skid Row foundling Seymour Krelborn (RICK MORANIS) has a heart-to-heart talk with Audrey II, the Venus people-trap he discovered during a total eclipse of the sun.

While her owner Seymour (RICK MORANIS) is briefly distracted, Audrey II, the vegetable vampire, prepares to wrap her lips around an early lunch.

Seymour (RICK MORANIS, left) and Audrey (ELLEN GREENE, right) find true love with the help of Audrey II.

Awkward orphan Seymour (RICK MORANIS, left) and beautiful lacking-in-confidence Audrey (ELLEN GREENE) fall in love and dream of a better life beyond Skid Row.

Dr. Orin Scrivello (STEVE MARTIN) is a peculiar dentist who can always find an opening to inflict pain — or at least give it his worst shot.

As Dr. Orin Scrivello, STEVE MARTIN is a deranged dentist by day and the hard-riding "leader of the plaque" at night. But to Audrey II, the botanical co-star of the Warner Bros. comedy, he's something else — suppertime!

FEED ME
(GIT IT)

Words by
HOWARD ASHMAN

Music by
ALAN MENKEN

Moderately bright

night long. _____ *That's right,___ boy!*

You can do it! _____ Feed me, Sey -

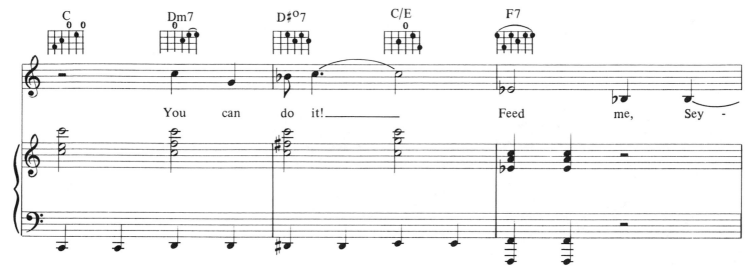

mour. _____ Feed me all _____ night long. _____

'Cause if you feed me, Sey - mour,

I can grow up big and strong.

Would you like a Ca - dil - lac car?
Would you like to be___ a big wheel,

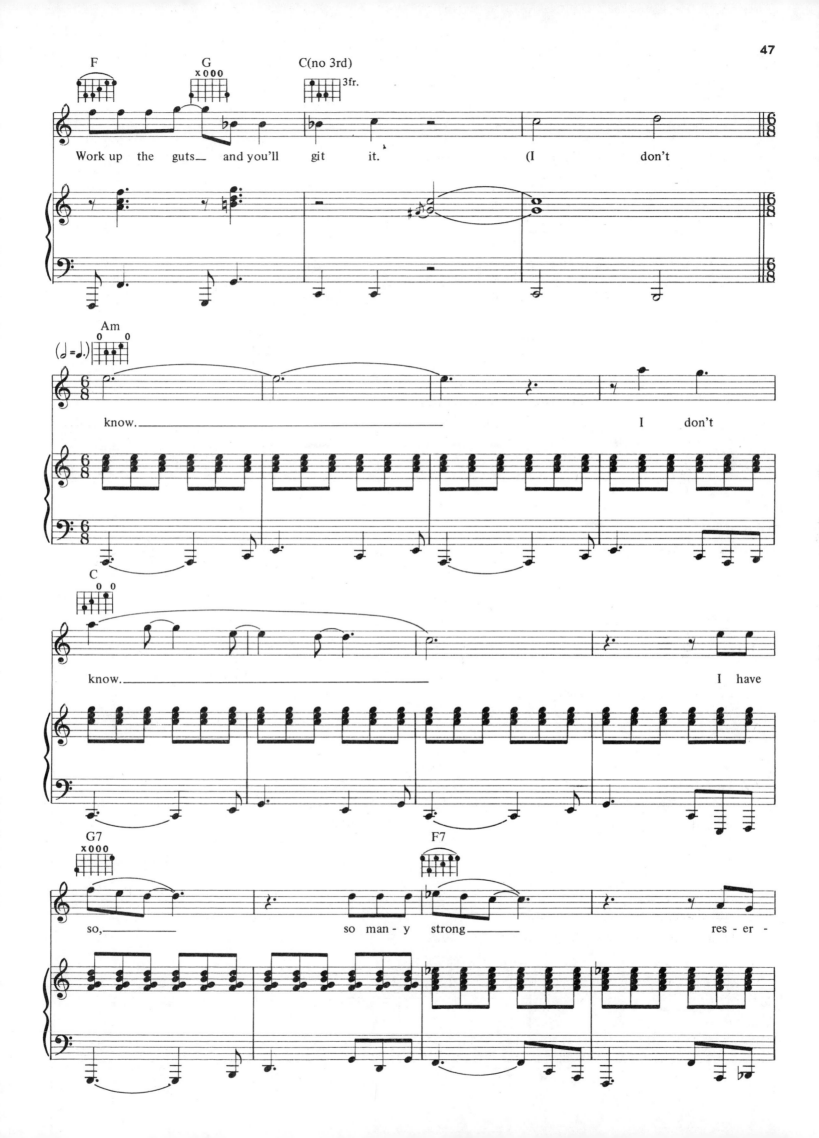

va - tions. _____

Should I go _____ and per -

form

mu - ti - la - tions?)

is-n't ver-y hard to see.___ Stop and think___ it o-

ver, pal.___ The guy sure looks like plant___ food to me. The

guy sure looks like plant___ food to me. The guy sure looks like plant__

___ food to me._____ He's so nas - ty,

SUDDENLY, SEYMOUR

Words by
HOWARD ASHMAN

Music by
ALAN MENKEN

Moderately bright

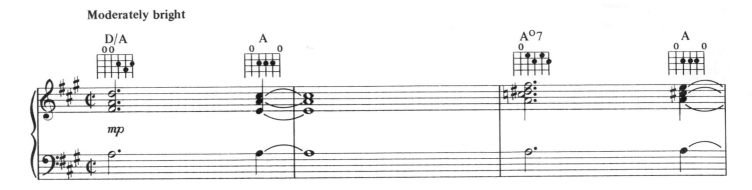

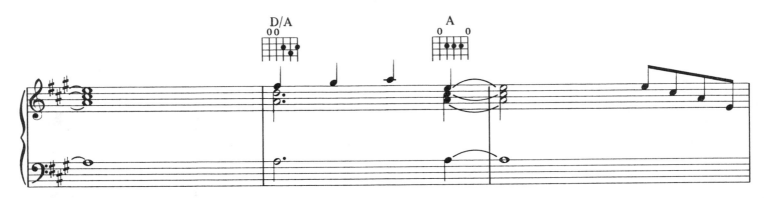

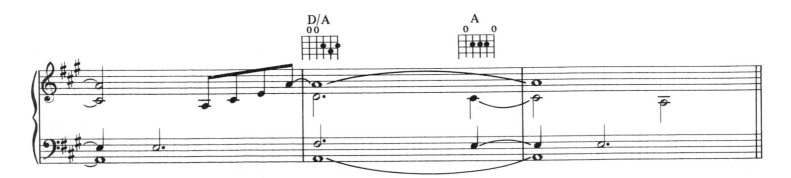

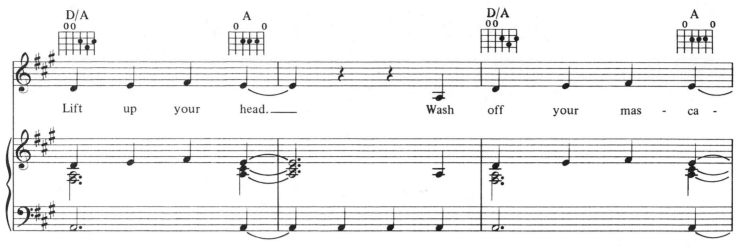

Lift up your head.___ Wash off your mas - ca -

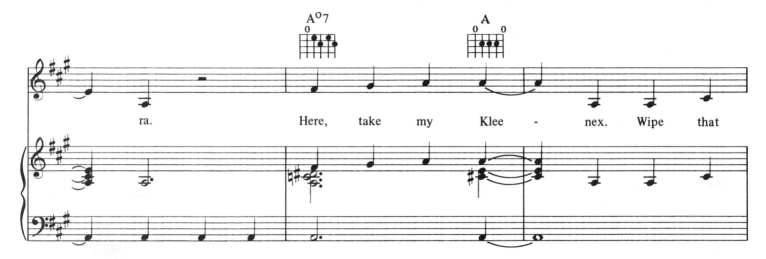

ra. Here, take my Klee - nex. Wipe that

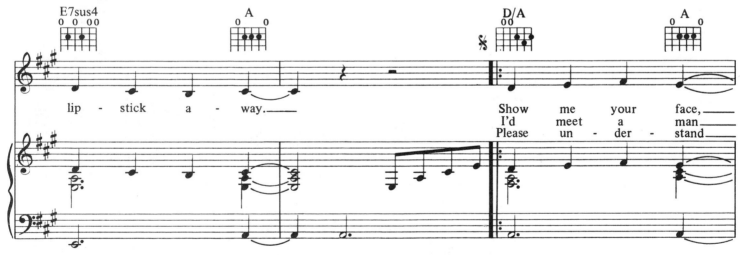

lip - stick a - way.___ Show me your face,___
I'd meet a man___
Please un - der - stand___

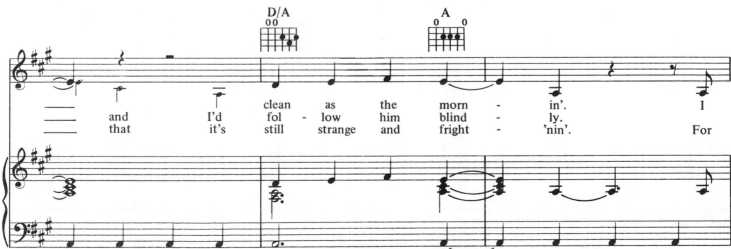

___ and I'd clean as the morn - in'. I
___ that I'd fol - low him blind - ly.
that it's still strange and fright - 'nin'. For

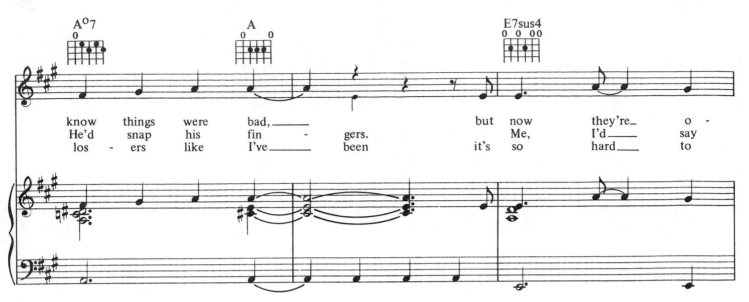

know things were bad,_____ but now they're_ o -
He'd snap his fin - gers. Me, I'd_____ say
los - ers like I've_____ been it's so hard_____ to

kay._____
"sure."_____
say:_____

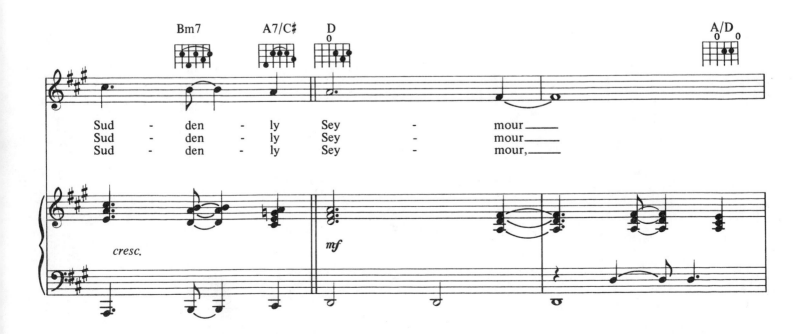

Sud - den - ly Sey - mour_____
Sud - den - ly Sey - mour_____
Sud - den - ly Sey - mour,_____

cresc.   mf

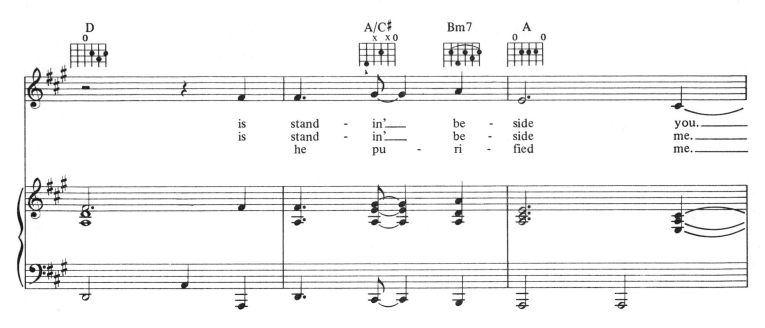

is stand - in'___ be - side you.___
is stand - in'___ be - side me.___
he pu - ri - fied me.___

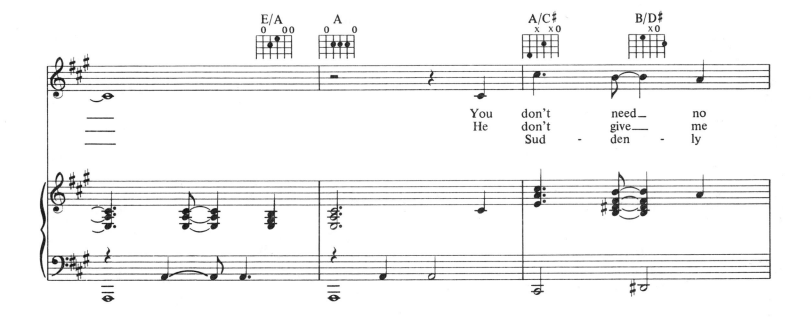

You don't need___ no
He don't give___ me
Sud - den - ly

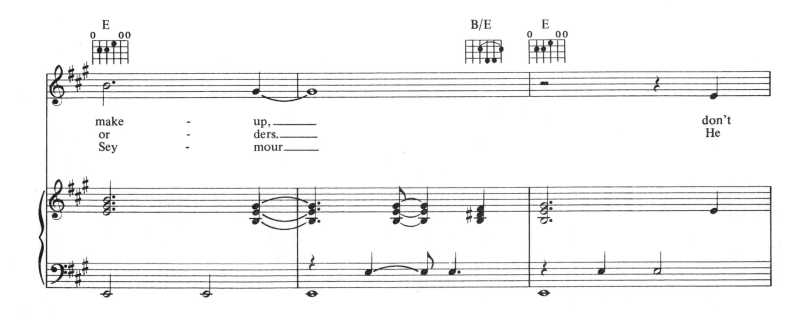

make - up,___
or - ders.___
Sey - mour___

don't
He

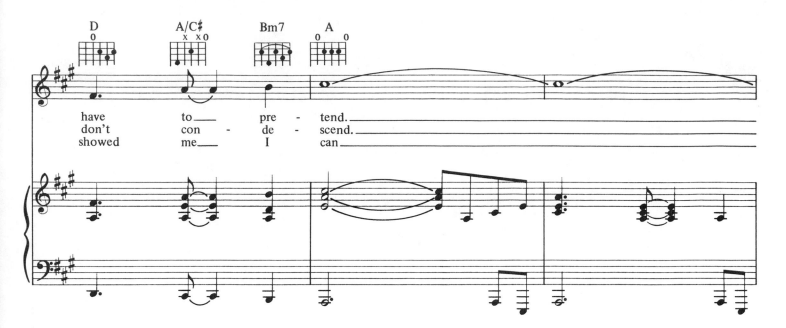

have to___ pre - tend.___
don't con - de - scend.___
showed me___ I can___

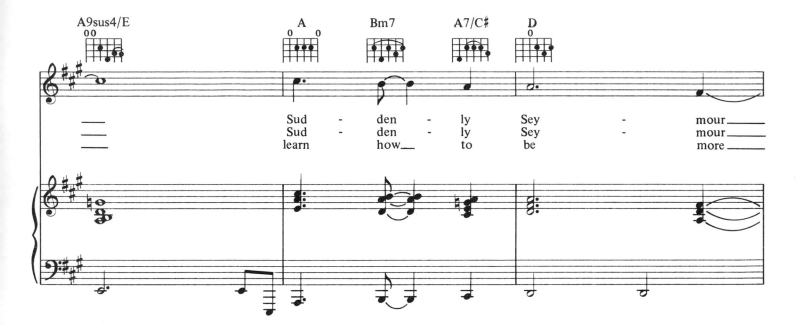

___ Sud - den - ly Sey - mour___
___ Sud - den - ly Sey - mour___
___ learn how___ to be more___

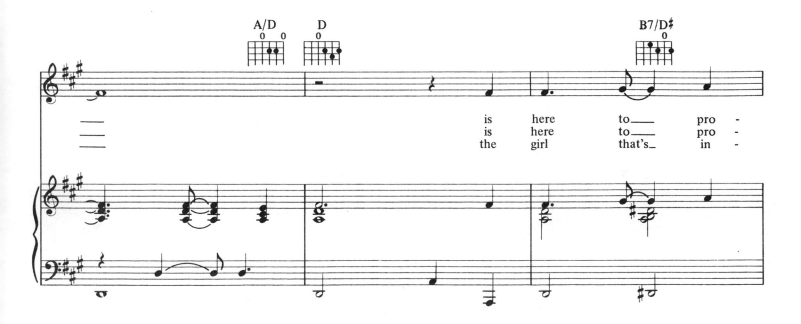

___ is here to___ pro -
___ is here to___ pro -
___ the girl that's___ in -

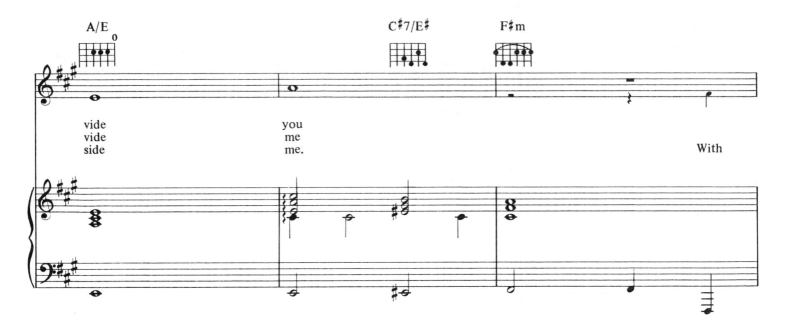

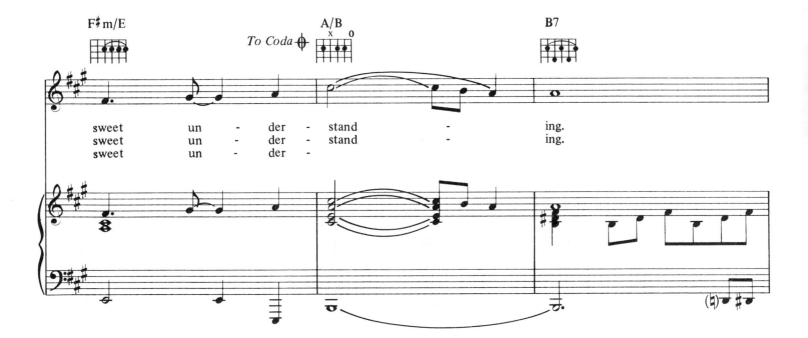

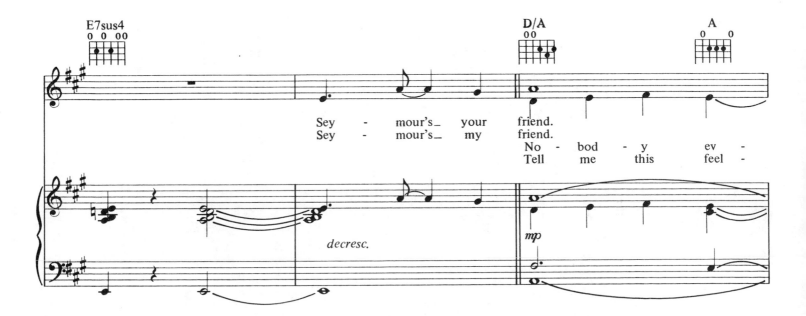

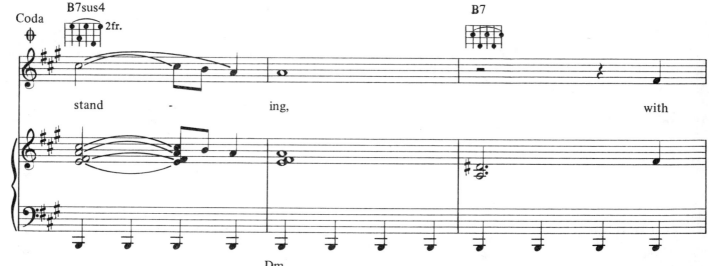

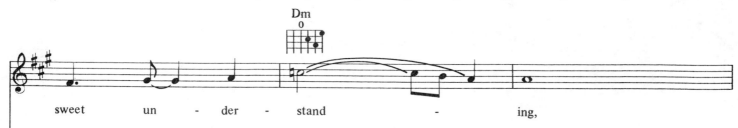

SUPPERTIME

Words by
HOWARD ASHMAN

Music by
ALAN MENKEN

you've got no - where___ to run.___

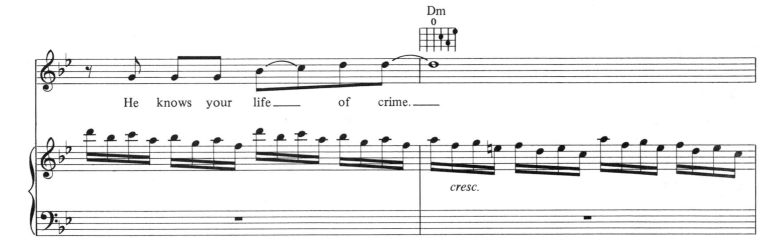

He knows your life___ of crime.___

cresc.

(scream) I think it's sup - per - time.___

Come on,___ come on,___ (spoken) think a - bout all___ those of - fers.___

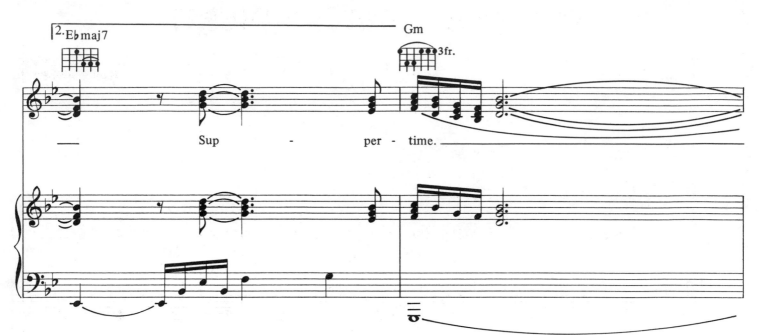

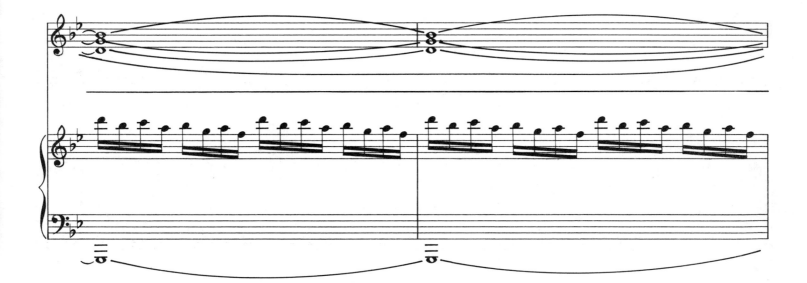

THE MEEK SHALL INHERIT

Words by
HOWARD ASHMAN

Music by
ALAN MENKEN

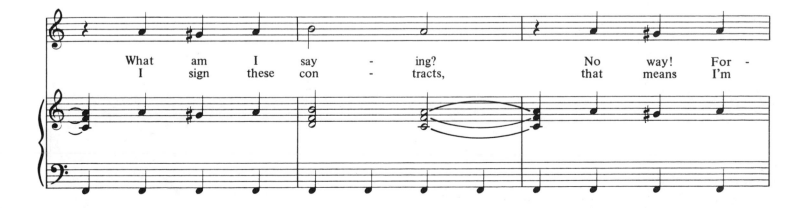

You know the meek are gon - na get what's com - in' to 'em, you know the meek are gon - na

get what's com - in' to 'em, you know the meek are gon - na get what's com - in' to 'em

by _____ and _____

by. _____

MEAN GREEN MOTHER FROM OUTERSPACE

Words by
HOWARD ASHMAN

Music by
ALAN MENKEN

To Coda ⊕

and   I   am___   bad.
and   I   am___

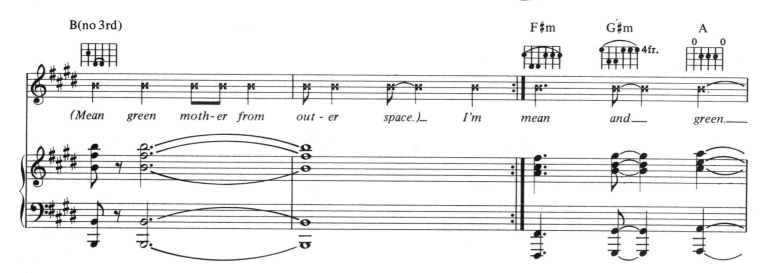

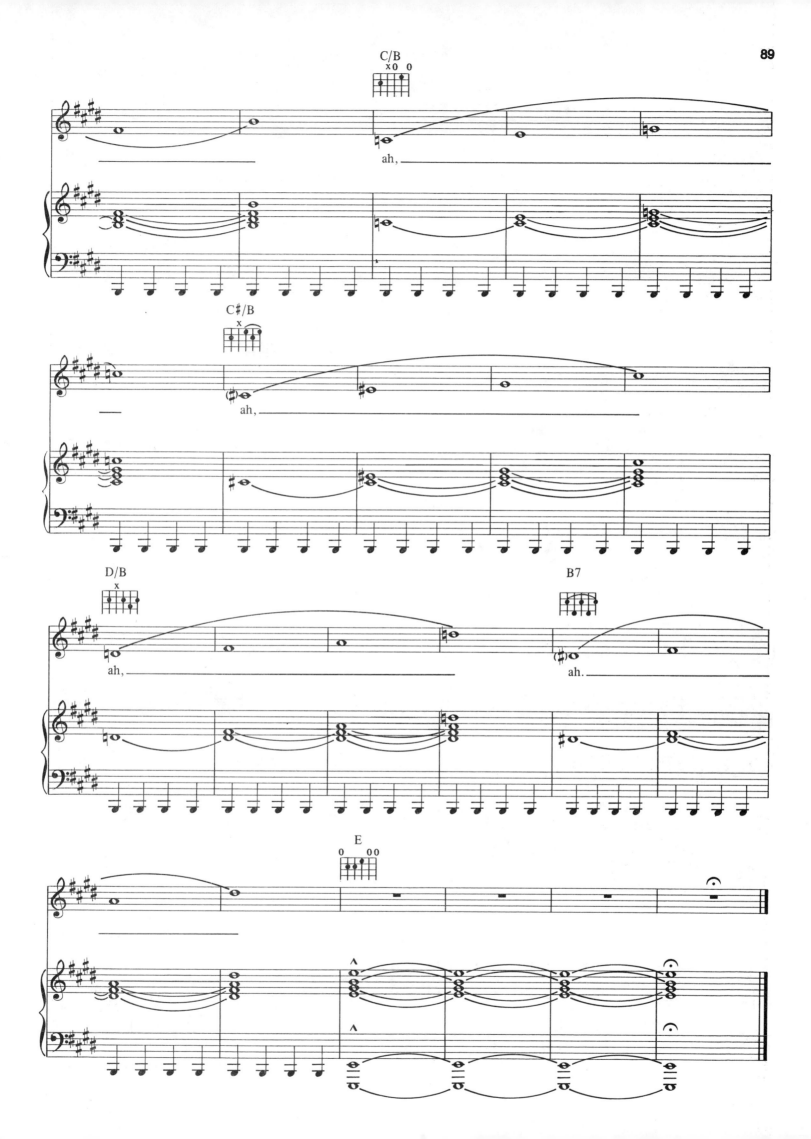

FINALE
(DON'T FEED THE PLANTS)

Words by
HOWARD ASHMAN

Music by
ALAN MENKEN

RICK MORANIS stars as Seymour Krelborn whose odd potted plant becomes a blood-sucking succulent in Warner Bros. "Little Shop of Horrors."

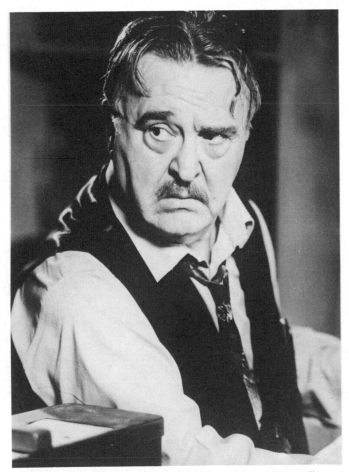

Skid Row florist Mushnik (VINCENT GARDENIA) has a dying business until a strange new plant draws customers in droves — and turns his store into a "Little Shop of Horrors."

Brave, blonde Audrey (ELLEN GREENE) dreams of a better life beyond Skid Row. Greene re-creates her starring stage performance in the monster musical about Audrey II, a man-eating plant.